Extinction Planet

ANNA CLAYBOURNE

W

FRANKLIN WATTS
LONDON • SYDNEY

Franklin Watts
First published in Great Britain in 2022 by the Watts Publishing Group
Copyright © the Watts Publishing Group 2022

Editor: Julia Bird
Designer: Rocket Design (East Anglia) Ltd

Alamy: Aldona Griskeviciene 8tc; Nature & Science 5tr; Stocktrek Images Inc. 8c;
Bjorn Svensson 36bl, Xinhua 39t.
Dreamstime: Leonello Calvetti 9bl.
Getty Images: Keren Su 38bl
Science Photo Library: Henning Dalhoff 6bl.
Shutterstock: A7880S 9c; Aghadhia Studio 37b; Anatolir 14cra; Ardea Studio 24-25bg, 33t; Adri-ana Margarita Larios Areliano
30r; AyselDesign 7cr; Angelina Bambina 27t; Tabitha Banu 6cra, 22tl; Si Berry 29bl; Berunin 5tlc; Blue Ring Media 8tl; Bianca
Botha 21t; Marcel Brekelmans 31t; Sly Browney 23br; Catmando 9bcl; Ira Che 24c; ClassicVector 14br, 37t, 41b; Crazy nook
7tl; Cu-riousity 29c, 29br; Irina Danyliuk 40cr;Si Dasha 30bl; Design9900 7tcl; Dibrova 39r; Didis 7br; Dream_master 32cra;
Antonina Dvorkina 23tr; H Elvin 14cl; Everett Collection 25t;Fancy Tapis 8tr; flowersmile 32cr; FOS-ICON 32br; GoodStudio 3br, 7tr,
10t,15,16cl, 20c, 20b, 40cl; Stephan Hawks 30cl; Hennadai H 14tr; Ideyweb 9bcr; Incomible 7c, 14c; Iscomit 41bl; Jeronim777
35t; Aleksandr Kariakin 13bl; R Kathesi 28-29bg; Katrinsav 28-29bg; Keikona 15t; Klyaksun 12-13bg; Andrew Krasovitcki 38cr;
Lainspiratriz 36-37b;Lightkite 33 b bg; Darya Lisavenka 19tl; Anton Lo-patin 11bl; Love Media Lab 26bl; Macrovector 32bg;
Maquiladora 27bl, 28cr; Magicleaf 1, 14cr; Tetiana Mal 34t; Joe McDonald 26br; Mintoboru 14cla; Morphart Creation 12bl, 12br;
Mspoint 22cl; Na_Studio 18cb, 28cl; Nadya Art 9br, 28bl, 38tr; Maryia Naidzionysheva 19b; Hiroyuki Nakai 11t; Nataleana 1bg;
Naoki Nishio 5br, 17b; NotionPic 6br; NTL Studio 40br; Oceloti 4-5bg,18-19bg t, 34tl; ONYXprj 21bl;N Pavel 28br; PavloArt Studio
13c; PCH Vector 6tr; Peiyang 16cr, 22-23cs; Persalius 4br; PixelChoice 3bl, 12cl; Olga Pogorelova 22bl, 27bc; Pretty Vectors 13br;
Lev Radin 34b; Matyas Rehak 30t; Ridackan 32cl;Rolandtopar 19c; Michael Rosskothen 4b; Rvector 6cr; Lana Samcorp 40bl;
Mary San 19tr;Leonel Serrano 21br; Shanvood 25b; Egor Shilov 23bc; Ama-nita Silvicora 40tl; SkyPics Studio 7tcr; SofiaV 2; Soyon
38l; StockSmartStart 41cl; StonePictures 38-39 bg;Irina Streinikova 43t; Studioworkstock 5tl, 41t; Sunny_nsk 33b; Supryiya07
23cr;Mascha Tace 29t; Tartila 17tl, 41cr; Tasty Cat 34c; Suniyo Tataisong 18-19c;Tgart2d 3tr, 26-27 bg; Tomacco 3tl,14tl; Uncle
Leo 42-43 bg; Usagi-P 16b;Sofia V 36t; Valeo5 14bc; vasek-vector 32tl; Vector Plotnikoff 17tr; VectorPot 6bra; Vector show 42c;
Veleri 32tr; Venimo 18-19bg b; Vir-inaflora 31b; White Space Illustrations 11br.Wikimedia Commons: California Academy of
Science, CCA 4.0 International 11c; Smith609, CC A 3.0 International 4t; Wellcome Library CCA 4.0 International 24b.

HB ISBN 978 1 4451 8174 5
PB ISBN 978 1 4451 8175 2

Printed in Dubai

Franklin Watts
An imprint of
Hachette Children's Group
Part of the Watts Publishing Group
Carmelite House
50 Victoria Embankment
London EC4Y 0DZ

An Hachette UK Company
www.hachettechildrens.co.uk
www.franklinwatts.co.uk

Contents

Gone forever

Millions of animals, plants and other living things live in our world. But for every species, or type of living thing, on Earth today, there are hundreds more that no longer exist. They have died out, or become extinct.

WHAT HAPPENED?

Life has existed on Earth for billions of years and it has changed over time. New species develop, or evolve, while others struggle to survive and become extinct. This is a normal, natural process. All these creatures and plants, for example, died out long before humans existed.

Cooksonia, an early flowering plant

DIED OUT 393 MILLION YEARS AGO

Paraceratherium, a ginormous, long-necked rhino

DIED OUT 25 MILLION YEARS AGO

At about 7.5m long, Paraceratherium was one of the biggest land animals ever

Here's a human to scale!

Tully monster, a small, strange sea creature with eyes on stalks and a long snout

DIED OUT 300 MILLION YEARS AGO

FOSSIL FINDS

We know about the extinct living things of the past because of fossils. These are traces or shapes left in the ground by the bodies of living things after they die.

Tully monster fossil

PE60343

EXTINCTION EMERGENCY!

Today however, there's a big problem. Living things are dying out much faster than they used to, thanks to our own species: humans. Hunting, pollution, farming and other human activities have already wiped out thousands of species and many more are endangered, or at risk of becoming extinct.

The dodo was a large, flightless bird. It died out in the 1600s, after humans settled on its home island of Mauritius. They cut down the forests where dodos lived, and brought dogs, rats and other animals that hunted the dodos and ate their eggs, until they were extinct.

DIED OUT 350 YEARS AGO

THIS BOOK IS ABOUT HOW THIS HAPPENED, HOW WE'RE TRYING TO CHANGE IT AND WHAT YOU CAN DO TO HELP.

Life on Earth

HIPPOPOTAMUSES

No one knows exactly how or where the first life formed, but it took place about 4 billion years ago. That's a LONG time! Long enough for millions of different living things to evolve, and for most of them to go extinct.

HOW LIFE BEGAN

Scientists think a mixture of chemicals in the sea, or in a hot mud pool, combined to make the first, basic living thing. The first life form was a simple, single cell.

It could have looked something like this

TREE OF LIFE

Gradually, more and more living things evolved, including multi-celled plants and animals. New species branched off from old ones, a bit like the branches and twigs of a tree. Scientists describe this as the 'tree of life' or 'tree of evolution'.

KANGAROOS

BUTTERFLIES

SNAILS

JELLYFISH

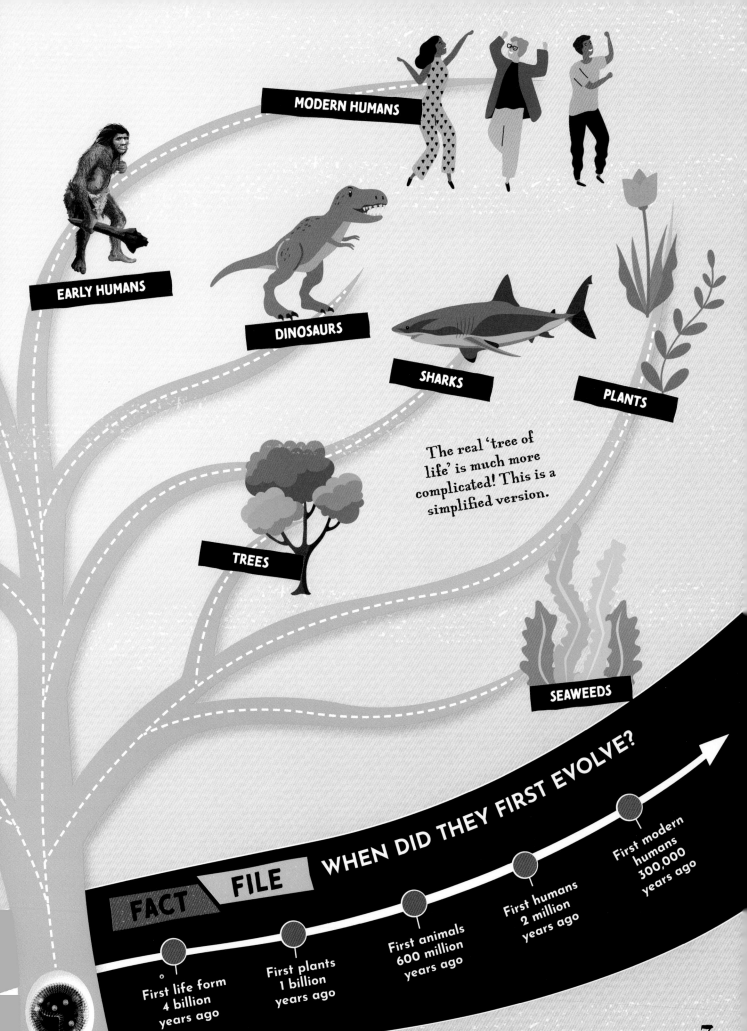

MODERN HUMANS

EARLY HUMANS

DINOSAURS

SHARKS

PLANTS

The real 'tree of life' is much more complicated! This is a simplified version.

TREES

SEAWEEDS

WHEN DID THEY FIRST EVOLVE?

FACT FILE

First life form
4 billion
years ago

First plants
1 billion
years ago

First animals
600 million
years ago

First humans
2 million
years ago

First modern
humans
300,000
years ago

Understanding species

Millions of species of living things have evolved, existed for a while, then died out. But what exactly is a species?

UNIQUE SPECIES

A species is a type of living thing. Species are different from each other because they have different genes. Genes control how living things work and what they look like. Let's take a close-up look at a giant squid.

Living things are made of tiny cells.

Cells contain genes, made of strings of a chemical called DNA.

The squid's genes give it its shape and abilities.

HOW SPECIES EVOLVE

Living things reproduce by making new cells that contain copies of their genes. These go on to become their offspring. During the copying, mistakes can happen that make tiny changes to the genes, which can change the living thing too.

If these changes are useful and help a living thing to survive, they continue to reproduce and so pass the new genes to future generations. This is how life changes and new species evolve.

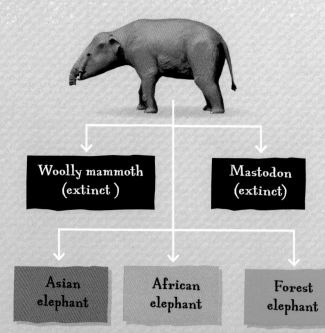

Woolly mammoth (extinct)		Mastodon (extinct)
Asian elephant	African elephant	Forest elephant

This family tree shows how several different elephant species evolved.

WHY DO SPECIES DIE OUT?

Species die out and become extinct for various reasons:

★ As more species evolve, they compete for food or living space, and some lose out.

★ An ice age or drought could make a species lose its food supply and starve.

★ A species is hunted to extinction by another species.

★ A natural disaster, such as a flood, wipes a species out.

ONCE IT'S GONE, IT'S GONE

As each species has its own unique genes, once a species has died out, it can't come back in the same way again.

The last sighting of a Chinese river dolphin was in 2004. It is now thought to be extinct.

Sometimes, a species changes so much over time that it becomes a new, different species. For example, some dinosaurs evolved into today's birds.

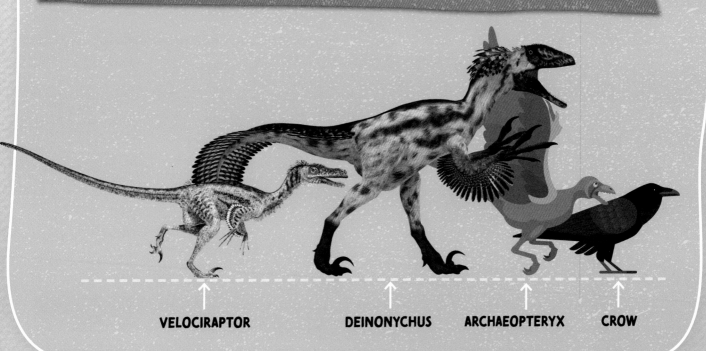

VELOCIRAPTOR   **DEINONYCHUS**   **ARCHAEOPTERYX**   **CROW**

The extinction rate

Today, extinctions are happening much faster than they used to. The extinction rate has been going up for several hundred years.

THE BACKGROUND RATE

The natural extinction rate, not counting extinctions caused by humans, is called the background extinction rate. Scientists think it should be about one species per year for every million species that exist.

There are probably around 8 million species on Earth, though we haven't discovered and named them all yet. So that means roughly eight species should be becoming extinct each year. Instead, scientists think 100, or even 1,000 times that many, are now dying out.

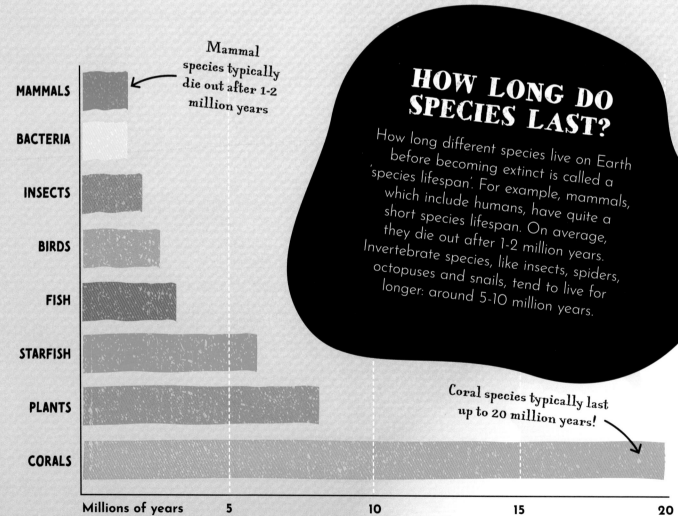

Mammal species typically die out after 1-2 million years

HOW LONG DO SPECIES LAST?

How long different species live on Earth before becoming extinct is called a 'species lifespan'. For example, mammals, which include humans, have quite a short species lifespan. On average, they die out after 1-2 million years. Invertebrate species, like insects, spiders, octopuses and snails, tend to live for longer: around 5-10 million years.

Coral species typically last up to 20 million years!

MAMMALS

BACTERIA

INSECTS

BIRDS

FISH

STARFISH

PLANTS

CORALS

Millions of years   5   10   15   20

SUPER-SURVIVORS

A few species manage to survive for much, much longer than average, and some of them are still around today. They are sometimes called 'living fossils'.

This unusual ant species, named Martialis huereka (meaning 'Martian discovery'), is thought to be 120 million years old.

The ginkgo tree has existed as a species for about 60 million years.

MASS EXTINCTIONS

Extinctions have not always happened at a steady rate. There have been several mass extinctions, when a huge number of species died out in a short time. They were usually caused by the Earth's climate heating up or cooling down a lot, or by natural disasters such as volcanic eruptions.

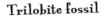

Trilobite fossil

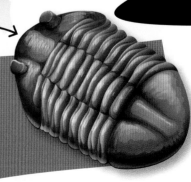

Trilobites were ancient sea creatures. The last trilobites died out in the Permian mass extinction, 251 million years ago.

No more dinosaurs

The most famous mass extinction was the K-T extinction, around 66 million years ago. It killed off the dinosaurs, as well as thousands of other species.

WHAT HAPPENED?

Scientists are still arguing over exactly what caused this mass extinction. The main theory is that a massive asteroid hit the Earth. Besides causing killer tsunamis, it blasted rock and dust high into the sky, which went into orbit, blocking out sunlight.

We know about the K-T mass extinction from layers of fossils in the ground.

After the extinction, the fossils are smaller and there are fewer of them.

IT WAS GOODBYE TO...

QUETZALCOATLUS
THE BIGGEST FLYING REPTILE EVER

PLESIOSAURS
SUCH AS ARISTONECTES

TREE-LIKE CYCADEOIDS

Rocks from about 66 million years ago contain a lot of iridium, a chemical that comes from asteroids

Some scientists think the main cause was huge volcanic eruptions in India, which released large amounts of gas and dust. Others disagree, saying that it could have been a mixture of causes.

WORLDWIDE DISASTER

Whether it was an asteroid strike, volcanic eruptions or something else, the debris blocked out the sunlight, killing a LOT of plants. Plant-eating animals, and the meat-eaters that hunted them, ran out of food. As well as dinosaurs and pterosaurs, sea creatures such as plesiosaurs and ammonites also went extinct.

The older, lower layers contain lots of dinosaur and sea creature fossils

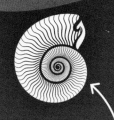

AMMONITES
SEA CREATURES RELATED TO OCTOPUSES, BUT WITH A HARD SHELL

MEAT-EATING DINOSAURS
SUCH AS TYRANNOSAURUS REX

... IN FACT, AROUND 70 PER CENT OF ALL THE SPECIES ON EARTH DIED OUT.

EXTINCTION TIMELINE

The K-T extinction was the most recent of five mass extinctions:

1 66 MILLION YEARS AGO (MYA)

K-T EXTINCTION

2 210 MYA

TRIASSIC-JURASSIC EXTINCTION

3 251 MYA

PERMIAN-TRIASSIC EXTINCTION

4 365 MYA

DEVONIAN EXTINCTION

5 440 MYA

ORDOVICIAN-SILURIAN EXTINCTION

NUMBER SIX?

Some scientists say the high extinction rate today means Earth is going through its sixth mass extinction - and this time, it's caused by humans.

We're all in this together!

Of course, it's sad when a species dies out and is gone forever. But that's not the only reason why the increasing extinction rate is a problem.

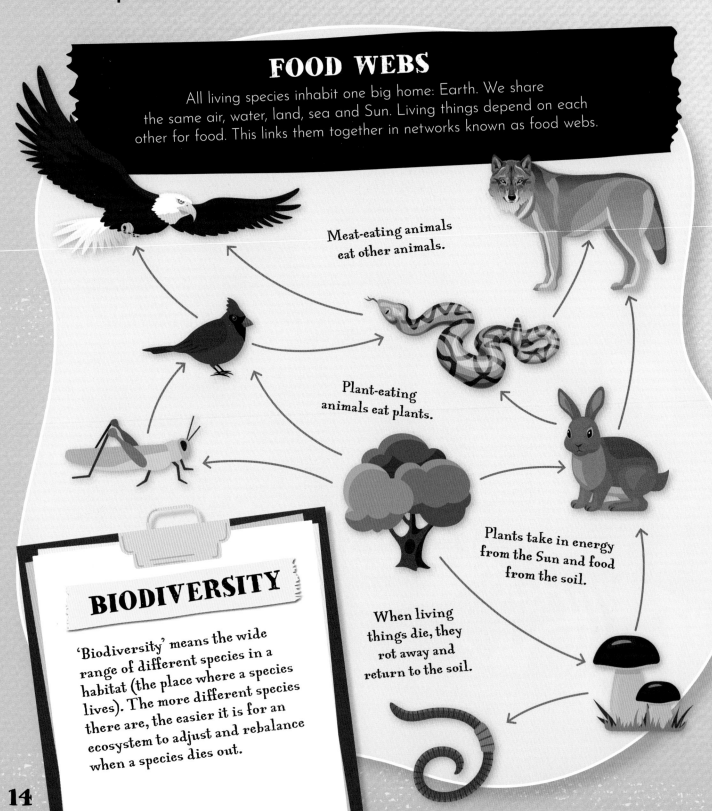

FOOD WEBS

All living species inhabit one big home: Earth. We share the same air, water, land, sea and Sun. Living things depend on each other for food. This links them together in networks known as food webs.

Meat-eating animals eat other animals.

Plant-eating animals eat plants.

Plants take in energy from the Sun and food from the soil.

When living things die, they rot away and return to the soil.

BIODIVERSITY

'Biodiversity' means the wide range of different species in a habitat (the place where a species lives). The more different species there are, the easier it is for an ecosystem to adjust and rebalance when a species dies out.

ADAPTATION

Over time, species evolve to suit their habitats. That's why, for example, the owl butterfly is camouflaged to match tree trunks in the forest where it lives.

But it also means that if a species loses its habitat, it may not be able to survive. So, for example, when a forest is cut down for farmland, its living things can die out.

ECOSYSTEMS

Living things and their habitats form an ecosystem. The whole world makes up one giant ecosystem. There are also smaller ecosystems within it, such as forests, rock pools or coral reefs.

If one species in an ecosystem dies out, it affects the other species too. They might have to find a different type of food, or become extinct themselves. When extinctions happen slowly the ecosystem can adjust. But when a lot happen all at once, it has a much bigger effect.

A coral reef is an ecosystem, with corals, fish, sharks, turtles, starfish, sponges, octopuses, seagrass and many other living things.

Extinction and humans

So if humans started out similar to other animals, how did we end up taking over so much of the world, and causing problems for so many other species?

THE HUMAN STORY

The first humans evolved in Africa, from apes who had switched from living in trees to walking on two legs. Over time, we changed a lot more...

2 MILLION YEARS AGO

Early humans began spreading around the world.

2.6 MILLION YEARS AGO

Our ancestors made and used stone hammers and knives.

FACT FILE

HUMANS HAVE...

★ Taken over 80% of Earth's wild land

★ Cut down 50% of the forests

★ Hunted at least 800 species to extinction.

HUMAN SPECIES

There have been several different species of humans, but most of them are now extinct. Modern humans, or Homo sapiens, are the only species left.

HOMO HABILIS

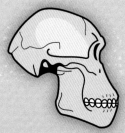

HOMO ERECTUS

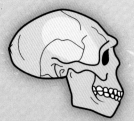

HOMO NEANDERTHALENSIS

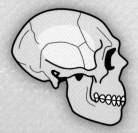

HOMO SAPIENS

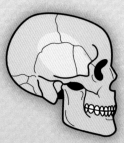

1 MILLION YEARS AGO

Humans learned to use fire for cooking and keeping warm.

12,000 YEARS AGO

Humans began farming, growing crops and keeping animals for food.

THE BIG CHANGE

Farming changed human history and paved the way for our modern lifestyle. People began settling down and building towns next to their farms. As farming provided more food, the population increased. We took over more and more wild land for ourselves, damaging natural habitats. We also kept on hunting and fishing, to feed more and more people.

GIANT MOA

Flightless birds called moas once lived in New Zealand. After humans first settled there around the year 1300, they hunted the moas to extinction within 200 years.

WHY ARE WE LIKE THIS?

Why did all this happen? There could be several reasons.

★ Human are brainy and good at inventing new things.

★ Walking on two legs leaves our hands free for making things and using tools.

★ Language helps us swap ideas and work in groups.

17

Steller's sea cow

Around 300 years ago, a giant cow roamed the chilly Bering Sea in the northern Pacific Ocean. Not a four-legged cow, but a sea cow, a massive sea mammal that was 9-10 metres long.

STORY OF A SHIPWRECK

In 1741, a ship exploring the northern Pacific was wrecked on a small island, and the survivors had to spend an icy winter there. They included German scientist Georg Steller, who studied the local wildlife. He described a big, slow-moving, seaweed-eating creature, previously unknown to science. It became known as Steller's sea cow.

Steller's sea cow was a sirenian, related to dugongs and manatees.

HUNTED TO DEATH

To stay alive, the sailors hunted and ate sea cows and other animals. After they escaped the island, Steller's journals were published, and people read about the new species. Soon, sailors began to catch more and more sea cows for food. Just 30 years later, Steller's sea cow was extinct.

It was much bigger than its closest relative alive today, the dugong (shown here to scale).

MORE EXTINCTIONS

Many other species have gone extinct in the last few hundred years, including...

TASMANIAN TIGER

(Thylacinus Cynocephalus)

A stripy dog-like marsupial from Australia, related to kangaroos.

Died out: 1936

GREAT AUK

(Pinguinus Impennis)

A flightless seabird, hunted for its meat and downy feathers

Died out: Around 1852

ST HELENA OLIVE TREE

(Nesiota Elliptica)

A small tree from the island of St Helena

Died out: 2003

← Human to scale

FACT FILE

STELLER'S SEA COW

Latin name: Hydrodamalis gigas

Length: Up to 10 m

Weight: Up to 10,000 kg - twice the weight of an elephant

Diet: Kelp seaweed

ACCIDENTAL EXTINCTIONS

Of course, humans didn't set out to drive all these living things to extinction. In the past, people often just used or hunted other living things without thinking about it. But as more and more species died out, we began to realise there was a problem.

Too many people?

Humans are sometimes called a very 'successful' species. In biology, that means being good at surviving, and continuing to exist by having more and more babies. But can a species be TOO successful?

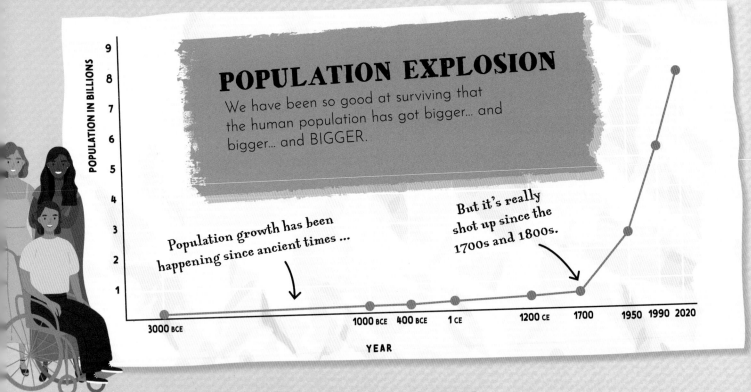

POPULATION EXPLOSION

We have been so good at surviving that the human population has got bigger... and bigger... and BIGGER.

POPULATION IN BILLIONS

Population growth has been happening since ancient times ...

But it's really shot up since the 1700s and 1800s.

3000 BCE   1000 BCE   400 BCE   1 CE   1200 CE   1700   1950 1990 2020

YEAR

WHY THE POPULATION GREW

The huge population boom of the last 250 years dates back to the Industrial Revolution (around 1760 – 1840). This was when we began making things in factories, using electricity and inventing machines and vehicles that used lots of fuel.

At the same time, we developed modern medicines, vaccinations and clean running water systems. People became healthier, wealthier and lived longer, leading to a global population of over 7.8 billion in 2021.

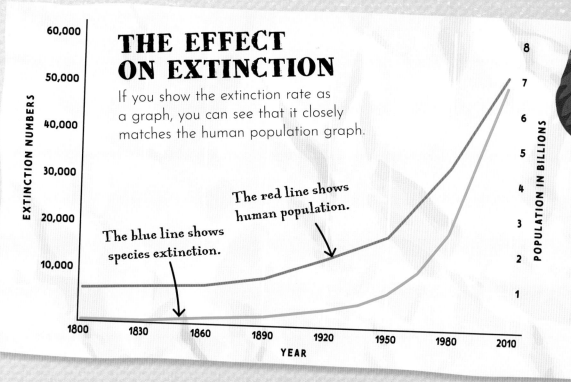

THE EFFECT ON EXTINCTION

If you show the extinction rate as a graph, you can see that it closely matches the human population graph.

The red line shows human population.

The blue line shows species extinction.

EXTINCTION NUMBERS

60,000
50,000
40,000
30,000
20,000
10,000

POPULATION IN BILLIONS

8
7
6
5
4
3
2
1

1800 1830 1860 1890 1920 1950 1980 2010

YEAR

The more humans there are, the more we affect other species. We take over more wild land, create more pollution and use up more resources.

But the population increase is now slowing down. Over time, we may be able to gradually lower the population again, so that humans are more in balance with nature.

Humans have used ivory from elephants' tusks since ancient times.

TWO NEW AGES

Humans have changed the world so much that we have created two new epochs, or time periods, in Earth's history.

THE HOLOCENE

The Holocene epoch (meaning 'totally new age') is the time since humans began farming, and developed cities and civilisations.

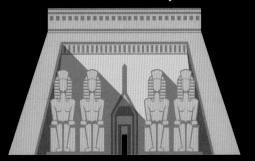

THE ANTHROPOCENE

The Anthropocene epoch (meaning 'new human age') is much more recent, dating from about 1950. In this epoch, we've changed the planet even more, with radiation from nuclear bombs, plastic pollution, space satellites and climate change caused by human activities.

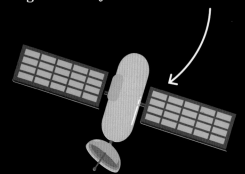

Threats to wildlife

Humans can harm other species in many different ways. Often, when a species dies out, it's because of a combination of these different threats.

HABITAT LOSS

The biggest cause of extinction is humans taking over wild habitats to build on or turn into farmland.

All three species of orangutan are at risk of extinction because the rainforests where they live are being cut down.

COLLECTING, HUNTING AND POACHING

Some people need to hunt animals or collect wild plant products to survive – but if we do this too much, species can die out. Even when hunting is banned, poaching, or illegal hunting, still happens.

Hunters often poach pangolins to sell their scales for making traditional medicines.

OVEREXPLOITATION

Overexploitation is when we use (or exploit) species faster than they can replace themselves. Overfishing is a common example.

Bluefin tuna are endangered because of overfishing.

NON-NATIVE SPECIES

When humans bring species like dogs or rats to a new area, they can change the ecosystem and cause extinctions.

New Zealand's kakapo is a flightless parrot. When human settlers brought dogs and rats with them to New Zealand, they hunted the kakapos, which are now endangered.

POLLUTION

Factories, mines, power stations, farms and car, lorry and plane engines can all release harmful pollution. Litter can kill wildlife too.

Sea turtles often mistake plastic bags for jellyfish and eat them, which can be deadly.

WAR

Bombs, tanks and fighting can destroy habitats and harm wildlife.

Snow leopards are at risk from land mines left behind after wars in the areas where they live.

CLIMATE CHANGE

Some types of pollution, called greenhouses gases, cause global warming. This is an increase in temperature which is changing climate and habitats around the world.

KNOCK-ON EFFECTS

Threats to wildlife are often interlinked. For example, war can lead to poverty, forcing people to hunt wild animals for food.

When corals get too warm, they become stressed and turn white, and sometimes die. This is known as coral bleaching.

Conservation

Over time, humans have realised how much damage we are doing. We're now trying to protect wildlife and wild habitats to save species from dying out. This is known as conservation.

LIVING WITH NATURE

In ancient times, many cultures understood the importance of treating nature with respect, and not using up resources. Old proverbs often contain these ideas...

Take only what you need, and leave the land as you found it.

Food will last while the forest lasts.

The frog does not drink up the pond in which it lives.

However, not everyone followed this advice, especially as societies became more modern and complex.

THE FIRST CONSERVATIONISTS

In 1662, writer and gardener John Evelyn wrote that too many trees were being cut down, and we should cut down forests sustainably – in other words, only as fast as they can regrow.

John Evelyn ⟶

All Nature is linked together by invisible bonds …

George Perkins Marsh

As the Industrial Revolution gained pace in the 1700s and 1800s, writers such as William Wordsworth and Henry Thoreau wrote about the importance of nature and wilderness. In 1864, George Perkins Marsh's book *Man and Nature* described how humans were changing the planet, and how all living things depended on each other.

New branches of science have developed to study conservation:

★ **ECOLOGY** The study of ecosystems, or groups of living things and their habitats.

★ **CLIMATOLOGY** The study of the climate and how it is changing.

★ **ENVIRONMENTAL SCIENCE** The study of the environment and our relationship with it.

MAKING CHANGES

Conservationists' ideas gradually became more popular and people began making changes.

★ The first wildlife reserves were set up in the 1800s.

★ In the 1900s, countries began passing laws to protect wild habitats and species.

★ Campaigners set up green political parties, and conservation charities, such as Defenders of Wildlife, Greenpeace and the World Wide Fund for Nature (WWF).

★ In 1962, Rachel Carson's book *Silent Spring* warned that pesticides used on farms were harming wildlife and ecosystems. Some were later banned.

Keeping track

If we want to save species from extinction, it's really important to monitor them. This means keeping track of how many of each species are left. This helps us to identify which species are endangered and work out how to help them.

THE IUCN

In 1948, countries from around the world set up the International Union for the Conservation of Nature (IUCN). It works with scientists, governments and campaigners to collect information on species and habitats, and to set up conservation schemes.

COUNTING SPECIES

Plants are easier to count because they stay still, but animals can be hard to find, especially rare endangered species. Scientists often use camera traps left in wild habitats. When an animal walks past, it triggers the camera to take a photo.

Camera traps are often fixed to tree trunks near paths used by animals.

This ocelot has triggered a camera trap and been caught on camera.

THE RED LIST

The IUCN keeps a list of thousands of species, called the IUCN Red List. It records as much information as possible about each species: where it lives, its population, any threats facing it and how endangered it is.

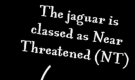

The jaguar is classed as Near Threatened (NT)

Each species is given a 'conservation status' or rating. The main categories are:

LC	Least Concern	Widespread and not at risk	e.g. Red-billed quelea
NT	Near Threatened	Likely to become endangered	e.g. Jaguar
VU	Vulnerable	High risk of becoming endangered	e.g. Koala
EN	Endangered	High risk of becoming extinct	e.g. Coast redwood tree
CR	Critically Endangered	Very high risk of becoming extinct	e.g. Brazilian guitarfish
EW	Extinct in the Wild	Only survives in captivity	e.g. Kihansi spray toad
E	Extinct	No individuals left	e.g. Steller's sea cow

FACT FILE

The IUCN lists almost 20,000 species as Vulnerable, Endangered or Critically Endangered.

CHANGING STATUS

The status of a species can change over time. Sometimes, a species becomes less endangered if conservation schemes are working and its population is increasing. For example, the giant panda's status was revised from Endangered to Vulnerable in 2016.

Endangered seagrass

You might not have heard of it, but seagrass is an incredibly important type of plant. It looks similar to normal grass, but grows underwater in shallow seas, forming seagrass 'meadows' on the seabed.

WHO NEEDS SEAGRASS?

We all do! Seagrass is an essential part of the ecosystem in shallow seas. Check out these seagrass superpowers!

Seagrass provides food for sea creatures such as dugongs and sea turtles.

It's an important habitat for sea creatures that live among the plants or between their roots, including seahorses, crabs, shrimps, sea snails, fish and jellyfish.

Seagrass holds seabed sand in place, protecting coasts from powerful waves.

SEAGRASS IN TROUBLE

There are over 60 different seagrass species, and almost a quarter of them are listed as near threatened, vulnerable or endangered. In the last 100 years, around 30% of the world's seagrass has disappeared because of human activities. Building sea walls, docks and harbours wipes out seagrass. Boats and fishing equipment scraping on the seabed can kill seagrass, and so can pollution that flows into the sea.

WHAT CAN WE DO?

The good news is that seagrass meadows can grow again quite quickly, in just a few years. So there are now seagrass replanting projects around the world. Teaching people about seagrass helps too, so they will try to avoid damaging it. Some seagrass meadows are protected in special marine reserves (see page 30), where fishing is not allowed.

A boat anchor like this dragging on the seabed can crush or uproot seagrass.

Like forests on land, seagrass meadows soak up carbon, helping to slow down climate change.

The fish and other animals living in seagrass meadows provide food for other animals, and sometimes humans too.

29

A safe place to live

Wild species are part of their ecosystem. They depend on their habitat and the other living things in it. To help a species survive, you need to protect its habitat and ecosystem as well as the species itself.

WILDLIFE RESERVES

A wildlife reserve is a protected area of natural habitat, set aside for wildlife. There are usually laws to stop people from building, hunting or harming wildlife in a reserve, to keep it as wild and natural as possible. There are wildlife reserves in all kinds of different habitats – forests, grasslands, deserts, icy Arctic tundra and coasts and seas.

This is Manuel Antonio National Park, one of Costa Rica's many wildlife reserves. It's made up of rainforest and coastline, and is home to several endangered species.

Northeast Greenland National Park

Greenland

HOW BIG?

The first modern wildlife reserve dates from 1821, when British explorer Charles Waterton built a wall around his house and a small area of nearby land to protect the trees and bird life. Today, some reserves cover huge areas of wilderness, such as the Northeast Greenland National Park, which takes up almost half of the country.

WILDLIFE WORKERS

Unfortunately, poachers often try to hunt animals, or collect endangered butterflies or plants, even in wildlife reserves. So most reserves have wildlife wardens who patrol the reserve to guard it from poachers.

Rangers look after orphaned rhinos in the Borana Conservancy wildlife reserve in Kenya, Africa.

KEEP IT GREEN

There are other ways to give wildlife places to live too, even in towns and cities:

★ Green buildings, with plant-covered balconies, ledges and rooftops

★ Wildflower meadows and wild areas in parks and gardens

★ Hedgerows made up of trees and bushes, used instead of walls and fences.

Wildlife laws

Most people know they shouldn't throw litter into the sea or hunt endangered species to eat, but somehow, these things still happen. This is why we need laws. There are now thousands of wildlife protection laws around the world.

TYPES OF LAW

Humans can harm or endanger wildlife in many ways. Laws have to ban or control a lot of different things in order to work.

HUNTING
There are laws that ban hunting endangered species, or limit the number of animals that can be hunted or caught.

COLLECTING
Some laws ban collecting endangered species from the wild – things like rare flowers, insects, birds' eggs, or animals to sell as exotic pets.

DUMPING WASTE
Laws exist to stop dangerous chemicals being released into the land, water or air.

LITTERING
Litter laws focus on requiring local governments to help people dispose of rubbish safely, as well as making sure there are bins for people to use and signs to direct them.

STARTING FIRES
In some places, laws ban people from starting fires that might cause wildfires and prevent people burning rubbish that will pollute the air.

TRADING
These laws protect against selling or buying items made from protected species – such as pangolin scales, tiger skins or rhino horns.

INTERNATIONAL LAWS

Countries usually make their own laws, including lots of laws to protect wildlife. But we also need international laws that apply around the world. These are especially important for sea creatures and the trade in endangered species, which cross country borders.

SAVING THE WHALES

For centuries, humans have hunted whales for their meat, bones and blubber. As the human population increased and new technology made whaling easier, we killed so many whales that some species almost died out.

In 1982, the International Whaling Commission, a worldwide organisation made up of over 80 countries, agreed to stop whaling to allow whale populations to recover. A few countries do still catch whales, but the ban has mostly worked well.

This graph shows how the population of blue whales fell to almost nothing, but has started to grow again.

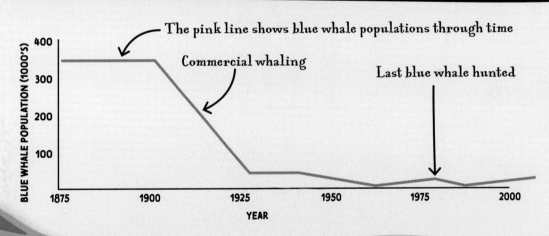

The pink line shows blue whale populations through time

Commercial whaling

Last blue whale hunted

BLUE WHALE POPULATION (1000'S)

400
300
200
100

1875   1900   1925   1950   1975   2000

YEAR

Blue whale

Spreading the word

One way to change the world is to help people learn about what's happening, and why it needs to change.

LEARNING AT SCHOOL

You've probably done projects about endangered species and habitats at school. Learning about these topics from an early age means you'll be aware of the problems, and what we can do about them, throughout your life.

A scarlet macaw, found in the rainforests of Costa Rica.

Costa Rica in Central America is a world leader in conservation. Learning about conservation is a big part of school lessons there.

ON TV

Another way to learn a lot about wildlife and the planet is by watching TV shows. They have helped millions of people to see how wild species are affected by things like plastic pollution and habitat loss.

The famous TV presenter and naturalist Sir David Attenborough has amazed and educated the world with his popular wildlife TV shows.

LEARNING THE FACTS

Sometimes having the facts can help people change their minds. For example, when people realise that buying ivory puts elephants in danger, or that a traditional medicine made of animal parts doesn't have any effect, they're less likely to want it.

Ivory items used to be much more common. Ivory was used to make ornaments, piano keys, snooker balls, and even false teeth! But now that most people know elephants are endangered because of poaching, this has changed.

SAFER SOLUTIONS

Learning new ways of doing things can help too. For example, farmers sometimes shoot elephants that eat their crops. But if they can switch to growing a crop that elephants don't like, such as mint, they can solve the problem in a different way.

CHANGING ATTITUDES

In these ways, cultures and attitudes change over time. Less than 200 years ago, hunting wildlife and collecting insects or birds' eggs were seen as normal. Now we know better, thanks to conservation campaigns and education.

SAVE HABITATS

STOP OVERFISHING

HELP NATURE

ONE EARTH

ENOUGH!

Ecotourism

Ecotourism means going to experience nature, or watch wildlife in its natural habitat, without bothering it or damaging the environment. It's a kind of tourism that can help both wildlife and people, as long as it's done carefully.

GOOD FOR ANIMALS

Wildlife reserves and national parks often run ecotourism trips and guided tours. They use the money they make to help run the reserve and keep it going. So you're not just getting to see amazing wildlife, you're helping to look after it too.

GOOD FOR LOCALS

Ecotourism also creates jobs for local people who can act as tour guides or work in the national park's ticket office, cafe or shop. It brings money into the local area and can also make people want to save and protect wildlife, instead of making money from hunting it.

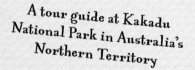

A tour guide at Kakadu National Park in Australia's Northern Territory

GOOD FOR TOURISTS

Visiting the world's wild places and seeing wildlife close-up can make tourists more interested in conservation, too. They learn about endangered species and want to help them. You might make more effort to avoid disposable plastic or stop leaving litter on beaches, for example, when you've seen ocean wildlife on an ecotourism trip.

WHAT'S THE PROBLEM?

Ecotourism can cause problems, though.

★ Building hotels and facilities for tourists can damage natural habitats.

★ Going on long journeys to see wildlife isn't very good for the environment, especially if you go by plane or car.

★ Too many visitors could scare wild animals or trample on plants, even if they don't mean to.

So ecotourism has to be carefully managed, with limited numbers, clear rules and as little disturbance as possible.

ON SAFARI

Long ago, 'going on safari' usually meant going on a journey to hunt wild animals. Now, it just means going to see them!

Wolong nature reserve

Wolong National Nature Reserve is a wildlife reserve in Sichuan, China. Although it's home to many plants and animals, it's most famous for its giant pandas.

PANDA KINGDOM

Wolong is sometimes known as the 'panda kingdom'. It's high in the Qionglai Mountains, an area of natural giant panda habitat with lots of bamboo, the panda's favourite food. About 150 wild pandas live in the reserve – probably 5-10% of the world's giant panda population. There are other endangered species in the reserve too, such as snow leopards, golden monkeys and the snow lotus flower.

Golden monkeys and snow leopards live in the reserve too.

Pandas prefer to live on steep slopes in cold mountain forests.

CAPTIVE BREEDING

As well as providing a protected home for wildlife, the Wolong Reserve has a world-famous captive breeding and research base, the Shenshuping Panda Centre. The centre helps pandas to have babies in captivity to increase their numbers. They can then be released into the wilder parts of the reserve.

Staff at Wolong have helped to breed more than 60 panda cubs.

PANDA NUMBERS

Wolong is one of over 40 panda reserves in China. Although there are still far fewer pandas than there used to be, the giant panda population is now starting to increase again.

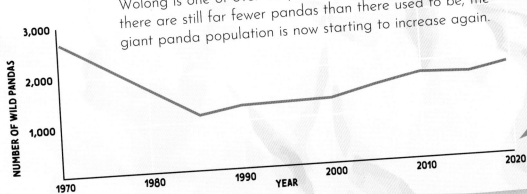

NUMBER OF WILD PANDAS

3,000

2,000

1,000

1970   1980   1990   2000   2010   2020

YEAR

FACT FILE

THREATS TO GIANT PANDAS

The giant panda is endangered for several reasons:

• Hunting for its fur, especially in the past

• Loss of its mountain forest habitat

• Habitat fragmentation, when a habitat gets broken up into smaller areas. This makes it hard for pandas to move around to find food and mates.

PANDA POWER

The giant panda is a type of bear but looks very unlike most bears. Its cute and cuddly appearance has made it famous around the world, and it's often seen as a symbol of conservation.

What can you do?

You might not get to see endangered plants or animals very often, but there are still lots of things you can do to help save endangered species.

DOS!

DO: Welcome wildlife by letting an area of your garden or school grounds grow wild.

DO: Support wildlife charities by joining them, raising money for them or adopting an animal in a zoo or reserve.

DO: Visit a wildlife reserve to support endangered species protection.

DO: Stick to paths and trails in the countryside, so you don't disturb animals or plants.

DO: Control your pets, especially cats and dogs, to stop them from catching wildlife.

DO: Use sustainable products, like wood from sustainable forests, recycled paper products and reusable water bottles.

DO: Use less fossil fuel by walking, cycling, switching to electric transport and saving energy at home, to help slow down global warming.

DO: Reduce, reuse, recycle - using less new stuff means fewer factories and farms, and less pollution.

BEANS

PASTA

DON'TS!

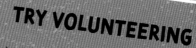

DON'T: Use strong weedkillers or pest-killing chemicals.

DON'T: Buy rare or endangered animals as pets, or items made from endangered species. Watch out for ivory, tortoiseshell and coral, as well as animal skins, fur and feathers.

DON'T: Drop litter anywhere, but especially on beaches, in water or in the countryside.

DON'T: Start fires in wild places.

DON'T: Use disposable plastic products, if you can avoid it.

DON'T: Bother, pester or touch wild animals, or pick wild plants.

DON'T: Buy food containing palm oil, unless it's certified as sustainable. Palm oil farming can destroy natural plant and animal habitats.

TELL OTHER PEOPLE!
Share your knowledge and encourage other people to follow the DOs and DON'Ts too!

TRY VOLUNTEERING

★ Help on a local beach clean-up or at litter-picking sessions.

★ See if you can volunteer at a local wildlife reserve.

★ There are even volunteering holidays, where you can do things like counting wild animals, setting up camera traps or planting trees.

Extinct planet?

Many scientists agree the world is facing its sixth mass extinction - in fact we're already in it. Can we fix it? And what if we can't?

CHANGING DIRECTION

It's already too late for Steller's sea cow (see pages 18-19), the dodo, the St Helena olive tree and the other species that humans have driven to extinction. Sadly, it may also be too late for many of the species that are now endangered.

Conservation efforts, such as setting up wildlife reserves, have already made a difference for some species. We just need to do a LOT more, as fast as possible, to keep wild habitats safe.

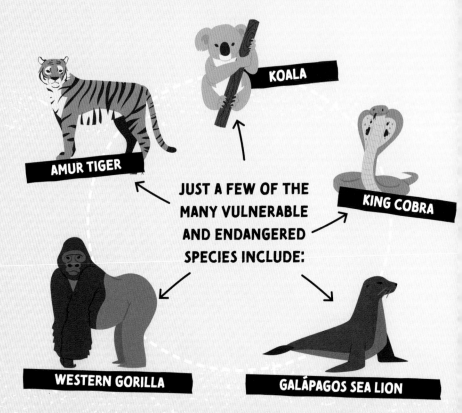

KOALA

AMUR TIGER

JUST A FEW OF THE MANY VULNERABLE AND ENDANGERED SPECIES INCLUDE:

KING COBRA

WESTERN GORILLA

GALÁPAGOS SEA LION

ARE NEW SPECIES EVOLVING?

After the last mass extinction, when the dinosaurs died out, lots of new species evolved to take their place. This could happen again, but it usually takes a very long time for species count to recover after a mass extinction: around 10 million years. As we've polluted the Earth and damaged habitats, it could take even longer.

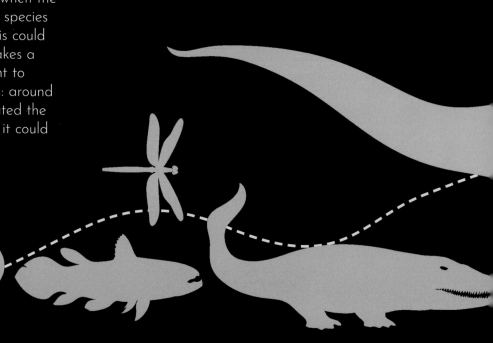

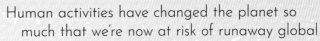

WHAT WILL HAPPEN NEXT?

Human activities have changed the planet so much that we're now at risk of runaway global warming causing rising sea levels, extreme flooding and other disasters, as well as the loss of biodiversity.

The average time a mammal species lasts is 1-2 million years, so we could be here until the year 1,500,000 or longer. If we keep harming the planet, however, human extinction could be a lot sooner.

★ TIME FOR ACTION! ★

We have to change, both for ourselves and for all the other species we share the Earth with. The good news is that we have all the tools we need to make these changes. Our ability to solve problems with new inventions means we can put our skills and knowledge into solving this one too. Listening to scientists and making everyday changes are the first steps on the road to recovery!

Glossary

Adaptation Changing over time to suit new or changed surroundings or conditions.

Anthropocene epoch A name for the most recent period in Earth's history, since about 1950, when human activities have dominated the environment.

Asteroid A small rocky object orbiting the Sun.

Biodiversity The variety of living things in a particular habitat, or in the whole world.

Carbon An element found in food, fuels and living things, which helps to form carbon dioxide, a greenhouse gas.

Camera trap An automatic camera that is triggered to take a photo when it senses movement. They are often used to monitor and count wild animals.

Cells The tiny units that living things are made up of.

Climate change A long-term change in Earth's climate patterns.

Conservation Efforts to protect and preserve living species and natural habitats.

Disposable Made to be thrown away after use.

DNA (short for DeoxyriboNucleic Acid) A chemical found in cells, used to encode instructions that make the cell work.

Ecosystem A particular area or place and all the living things that are found there.

Ecotourism Going to visit wild areas and watch wildlife as a holiday or day out.

Endangered At risk of dying out and becoming extinct.

Energy The power to make things happen or do work, found in various forms such as electricity, sound, light and movement.

Environment Our surroundings, in particular the natural world.

Environmental movement A political movement, originating in the 1800s, that aims to protect the natural environment, or surroundings.

Evolution A process of gradual change over multiple generations of living things.

Extinct An extinct species is one that has died out and no longer exists.

Extinction rate The amount of species per year that are expected to go extinct.

Food web A network of plants and animals in an ecosystem that depend on each other for food.

Fossil The remains or trace of a prehistoric living thing, preserved in rock.

Fossil fuels Fuels such as coal, oil and gas, formed underground from animals or plants that died long ago.

Genes Sequences of chemicals arranged along strands of DNA, which act as coded instructions for cells.

Global warming A gradual increase in Earth's average temperature over the last two centuries, caused by human activities.

Green A word used to mean aware of the need to reduce damage to the planet.

Greenhouse effect The way some gases in Earth's atmosphere trap heat, increasing global warming.

Greenhouse gases Gases that contribute to the greenhouse effect, such as carbon dioxide and methane.

Habitat The natural home or surroundings of a living thing.

Habitat fragmentation Natural habitats being broken up into smaller, separate areas.

Habitat loss The destruction of wild natural habitats.

Holocene epoch The name for the period of time since humans began farming, about 12,000 years ago.

Industrial Revolution A period of major development around the word, starting in the 1700s, towards using factories, machines, engines and electricity in manufacturing and transport.

Land mine A small explosive device hidden under the ground.

Mass extinction A period of extreme change on Earth which caused a large proportion of living species to become extinct.

Monitoring Keeping track of a wild species and checking on its numbers, health and movements.

Non-native species Species introduced to a new area from elsewhere, which can damage the local ecosystem.

Overexploitation Using too much of a natural resource in an unsustainable way.

Overfishing Catching too many fish, so that fish populations cannot recover and start to fall.

Poaching Illegal hunting.

Population The number of people or other living things in a place.

Sirenians A family of sea mammals that includes manatees, dugongs and the extinct Steller's sea cow.

Species The scientific name for a particular type of living thing.

Species lifespan The average time that a particular type of species, such as mammals or insects, survives for before dying out.

Sustainable Able to be continued in the same way over a long time.

Tracking Following the movements of a wild animal.

Tsunami A huge ocean wave that flows onto the land, caused by sudden movements in the sea.

Wilderness A wild, natural area that has not been damaged or taken over by people.

Wildlife reserve A wild area set aside for wildlife, and protected to stop it from being changed or damaged by humans.

Further reading

BOOKS

Awesome Infographics: Endangered Animals

By Harriet Brundle and Heather Kissock (AV2 Books, 2021)

The science, facts and figures of endangered species in amazing infographics.

Saving Species

By Jess French and James Gilleard (Wren & Rook, 2018)

Meet endangered species from around the world, and find out about the threats
that face them, as well as what is being done to help.

100 Endangered Species

By Rachel Hudson and Brett Westwood (Button Books, 2021)

Beautiful illustrations of 100 endangered species, along with science and conservation facts.

Extinct: An Illustrated Exploration of Animals That Have Disappeared

By Lucas Riera (Phaidon Press, 2019)

Discover all kinds of beautiful and unusual animals that have become
extinct in the past century.

Guardians of the Planet: How to be an Eco-Hero

By Clive Gifford and Jonathan Woodward (Buster Books, 2019)

How to help the planet with a wide variety of activities, projects and everyday habits,
from helping wildlife and cleaning up the coast to running a green home.

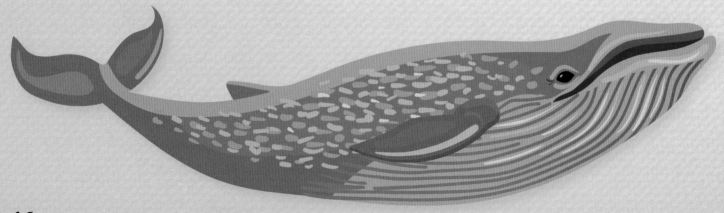

WEBSITES

support.wwf.org.uk
World Wide Fund for Nature conservation charity website.

www.iucnredlist.org
The IUCN Red List, where you can find out about all kinds of endangered species.

www.edgeofexistence.org
Edge of Existence, a conservation scheme helping a variety of endangered species.

www.fauna-flora.org
Flora and Fauna International, a global wildlife conservation organisation.

www.nationalgeographic.com/news/2016/11/bacteria-tiny-microscopic-shapes
Take a closer look at some germs and other microorganisms under a microscope.

WATCH

Planet Earth II. 2016
Nature documentary TV series presented by Sir David Attenborough, exploring the world's nature and wildlife and the impact of humans on the natural world.
Available on BBC iPlayer and Amazon Prime Video.

Extinction: The Facts. 2020
Documentary film presented by Sir David Attenborough, looking at the current mass extinction event, its causes and the effect on biodiversity.
Available on BBC iPlayer and Amazon Prime Video.

Index